GW00362522

THE SUPERNATURAL POWERS OF A PRAYING MAN

ARCHBISHOP N. DUNCAN-WILLIAMS

The Supernatural Powers of a Praying Man

Copyright © **NICHOLAS DUNCAN-WILLIAMS 2006**

ISBN 1-931130-5
For Further information, please contact:

The Office of the Archbishop
9759 Mountain Laurel Way
Suite 1B
Laurel, MD 20723
(240) 418-0808

Graphic Design & Printing
Cooray's House of Publications Sdn Bhd
Tel : 603 - 4270 3722 Fax : 603 - 4270 1733
Email : jncooray@streamyx.com

CONTENT

INTRODUCTION

This booklet was designed for the CHRISTIAN MAN. It will challenge, motivate, and draw you back on course to your real purpose as a man. I wrote this book to push you off the edge away from your comfort zone into the thick of the battle. The war began the very moment you confessed Christ Jesus as your Savior. There is war going on in the heavenlies over you family, church, community, city and nation, and the world around you. All men are called to effect change and to enforce the will of God into manifestation in these end times.

Prayerlessness is causing impotence in the realm of the spirit for men. The Bible commands us to pray without ceasing. What occurs when men do not pray ceaselessly? The product of such prayerlessness is what we see in our society today: sexual decadence, fatherless future leaders, lack of authority in our homes, our children killing each other...the list goes on. God is calling us to pray and to stand our ground, to take battle to the enemy's camp, and to retrieve everything the enemy has stolen from us. You are being controlled by Jezebel and Delilah; and, unless you take your proper stand, you might be overtaken.

This book is not designed to teach you how to pray. There are many good books out there which have already taught many of you how to pray. Rather, this book is designed to motivate you and reinforce <u>your need for prayer</u>. It is my prayer, when you have finished reading this book, you will have received an impartation to pray

Chapter One

AN EPIDEMIC

Remember the Ebola Virus? It is very likely you will not remember because this deadly virus was contained before it could reach the western world. The Ebola Virus is a type of viral hemorrhagic fever. The symptoms of this fever begin four to sixteen days after infection. Once the symptoms, which consist of fever, chills, headaches, muscle ache, and loss of appetite, begin, the disease can take out its victim in less than 72 hours. The progression of this disease is accompanied by vomiting, diarrhea, abdominal pain, sore throat, and chest pains. As the virus rapidly spreads, blood eventually fails to clot causing the patient to bleed from injection sites, the gastrointestinal tract, skin, and other organs. Take a moment to picture a victim of this disease. The host of the virus is unknown.

If you think the Ebola disease is terrible, consider further as I tell you about another type of outbreak in OUR CAMP. It affects the "head" and quickly spreads like the Ebola Virus, attacking and destroying the vital organs which keep our bodies functioning. This virus I call, "PWC," (Prayerlessness without Ceasing). It is in direct opposition to the command of Jesus that we <u>pray</u> without ceasing.

Unlike the Ebola Virus whose host is unknown, this virus "PWC" has several hosts-some of which are: busy schedules, indifference, and pride, to name a few. It is subtle and attacks from within and from without. It weaves a gradual web of deceit around its victim and spreads usually from the head to other parts of the body-in this case, the body of Christ.

The complicated weave of this web almost makes it impossible for one to free oneself once he is caught in its trap. The symptoms of this disease are so intricate, they almost go undetected. The virus PWC weaves itself into the very fabric of our worship. How can anyone speak about the imbalance in the church without acknowledging that the imbalance is caused by over-emphasis on worship, praise, faith, finances, and everything else but prayer? Am I suggesting that we could ever worship God enough? No, I am not. What I am saying is there is a critical need for corrected balance.

When the enemy attacks, you cannot sing him away. If he is attacking your children, or your emotions, or your finances, you cannot recite to him scriptures and expect him to flee. We are steadily losing our crucial and only connection to God-prayer. As leaders of the millennium church, we have placed undue emphasis on music, praise, worship, finances, great marketing strategies, and have ignored prayer. We have taught our men to worship, quote scriptures, to "name it and claim it," and have failed to teach them the core part of our Christian walk, which is praying. Prayer is the cord that keeps us connected to the Father, our Source. The imbalance we have created has produced a generation of lawless and prayer-less men.

THE TIME HAS COME FOR MEN TO RISE UP, TO GO BACK TO THE BASICS, AND TO LEARN HOW TO PRAY

THE DIAGNOSIS

The time has come for men to rise up, to go back to the basics, and to learn how to pray. There is urgency in the realm of the spirit for balance. If we are to make it through in these times, prayer is the key. The greatest form of power cannot be found in Viagra, in the gym, or in steroids; but it can be found in the man who has made prayer his secret habitation.

Such a man abides continually under the shadow of the Most High. He is covered. Show me a man who is a survivor of storms, and I will show you a man of prayer. How can two walk together unless they agree, and how can they agree unless they communicate?

Take, for example, a married couple. Tell me how they can survive without the fundamental requirement of communication in their relationship? Couples who do not share good communication are walking in frustration. They may have a two-million dollar house, with a fleet of expensive cars, and a billion-dollar business. However, if they lack good communication, their monumental wealth cannot save them. If you go inside the boundaries that protect the house, you will find a couple struggling to survive.

Or consider this: the mark of a great coach or leader is his ability to interact and communicate effectively with his team. He knows exactly what the team needs to be motivated, because he has taken time to know and understand them. Between any two persons the more effective communication is, the greater the bond they share.

THE CHURCH LACKS POWER BECAUSE MEN ARE NOT PRAYING AS THEY OUGHT

The church lacks power because men are not praying as they ought to. This fact is evident in our prayer meetings. Organize a prayer meeting, and women will fill your seats. (Then we wonder why women are taking on leadership roles in our homes.) We read books on prayer, get motivated to pray effectively for a day or two, and slip right back into prayerlessness. Why do we work sixteen hours a day, spend a couple of hours towards a workout, and commit <u>only sixteen minutes</u> in prayer?

No wonder the enemy is attacking our homes, churches, and our children. Yes, our children are killing each other while we look on helplessly. Our church leaders are fighting among themselves, and we are losing our sheep. Some leaders have resigned themselves to doctrinal debates. However, as we linger in our debates and whatever else that takes up our prayer time, the enemy gradually gains ground, dispersing his virus (demons, spirits) into our camps.

Let me provide a balance here so that you will not get me wrong. Praying does not always bring an automatic and sudden disappearance of problems, or overnight church growth, or tremendous success. You and I have been around long enough to know that storms come to everybody. Whether you prepare for them or not, storms are an integral part of our lives; and we just have to deal with them.

"No weapon fashioned against you shall prosper...
Isaiah 54:17

This scripture tells us that surely weapons shall be formed against us. However, even when they are, the weapons will not prosper in the destruction of the target they are sent to attack, <u>if we are standing in a position of prayer.</u> A praying man is a man who is able to withstand and survive the storms of life because when the storms come he is connected strongly to his source-God.

THE PRAYING MAN CHANGES
THE CLIMATE IN HIS CITY, TOWN, OR
COMMUNITY

The praying man changes the spiritual climate in his city, town, or community. The praying man's foreknowledge of the future enables him to strategize and establish a plan to combat the enemy's attack. An army that goes to war without a strategy is bound to lose. Consider what would happen if the viral infection of Jezebel or Delilah attacked you with voracious appetites of lust? Will you let the controlling powers of Jezebel hold you captive or the seductive powers of Delilah grip you in bondage? Will drugs be your way of escape? Watch out, man! The devil is after the head, and that is you!

YOU ARE THE PROMISE KEEPER AND THE SEED BEARER

You are the promise keeper and the seed bearer. Your position is an important one. This is not to say at all that the position of woman is not important. However, the head is an essential part of the body. It is in the region of the head that decisions are made and visions are conceived. When the head is badly hit, it affects the body in its entirety.

Chapter Two

THE VIRUS IN REVIEW

Wake up from your sleep! Wake up from your slumber! The alarm shrieks just as it did in the era of Adam and Eve when the enemy entered the garden to take what the Father had given Adam-his domain, his sphere of influence. Be alert, for your adversary the devil is going about like a roaring lion seeking whom he may devour. Why is he seeking prey? He is aware that a praying main will not succumb easily to his lies. So he roams to and fro seeking the man who is vulnerable, out of rank, and has made prayer a five minute affair.

"For we wrestle not against flesh and blood, but against principalities, against powers, against the rulers of darkness of this world, against spiritual wickedness in high places."
Ephesians 6:12

Principalities are princes of the underworld who manipulate certain sections of the universe. They are ruling spirits assigned over nations and cities. These spirits function by exerting their influence over heads of nations and kings. They seek to control the political lives of these nations, using the human head as their main device of operation. Principalities are the highest of the rankings in the enemy's domain.

Powers are the second level of authority in the devil's domain. They exercise their authority over the decision-making bodies of a nation, influencing the structures of the governing authorities, encouraging wickedness by promoting injustice, and controlling lawmakers and policy makers in places of authority in the land. In **Daniel 6:3, 6-8,** the counselors and governors conspired against Daniel and influenced King Darius to issue decrees banning all religious activities. This same spirit is ruling today, banning prayer in schools and much more. (I encourage you to take time to study the book of Daniel.)

Powers can also sway the thoughts and feelings of human beings. They have the power and capability of drawing Christians away from praying as much as they ought to, minimizing their compassion and concern for lost souls, etc. Another mode of operation for these powers is through the media. Their assignment is to make you believe lies.

Rulers of darkness, as stated in **Ephesians 6:12**, is derived from the Greek, *"kosmokrateros,"* which means "world rulers." These rulers of darkness are mandated by the devil to promote false religion and occult practices, thereby enslaving the souls of men in deception. The aim of the rulers of darkness is control. They will control anything they can lay their vile hands on. They deceive by false teachings, false visions, and dreams, etc.They promote horoscope, hypnotism, witchcraft, black and white magic, and many other forms of control.

The next level is spiritual wickedness. Their assignment is to promote lawlessness and wickedness in the land, ensnaring souls of men into all manner of abominable sins, such as homosexuality, rape, lust, lasciviousness, suicide, drug addiction, and more. Spiritual wickedness is responsible for tragedies. such as accidental deaths and suicides. In my book, **"Binding the Strong Man,"** I have painstakingly detailed the operation of the various demonic spirits and how we can break their powers.

YOU ARE IN A WAR!
LET US TAKE THE BATTLE TO
THE ENEMY'S GATE!

Men, this thing we are dealing with is serious. We are dealing with a well-organized cartel of evil. We cannot afford to put our women on the frontlines. You are in a war! Do not take anything for granted. The god of this world is working overtime, and you need to rise up and be in rank.

You are wrestling with unseen persons without bodies. You are warring against powers of this world and against spiritual wickedness.

Wicked spirits are foul, malicious spirits who operate without mercy. They destroy anything good and will destroy you and what is dear to your heart in no time if they can. So, Man of God, lift yourself up, get yourself out of your slumber state, put on your armor; and let us take the battle to the enemy's gate.

This virus of prayerlessness is not partial. It is an equal opportunity virus. It does not care whether you stand in the office of president or bishop, janitor or general. Its main purpose is to throw other activities, seemingly more pressing than prayer, your way. This PWC will weaken your mind first and trick you into believing that God is indifferent and understands your busy schedule. Just for reasoning purposes, God may understand; but, frankly, the devil does not care. He will hit anything, anytime, anywhere that will hurt your most. When things go wrong in your community, do not look on aloof; but grab your weapons of warfare and begin to fight.

The devil builds a web of deceit to fence you in. After the virus attacks your mind set, it begins to break your defenses. It moves in quickly with a strong spirit of lust-lust of the eyes. Greed and Pride are killers, and so is Lust. We as men have to deal with them daily. If you are honest, you will agree that what I am writing is true. Ego is a smart way of allowing the enemy to come in. Egotism is self-centeredness. It has a best friend by the name of Greed. Anytime you allow your ego to get in the way, greed is near by. You soon find yourself wanting more of everything. You make more than enough money, but you want more. An insatiable appetite is gradually growing within you.

You have a 20,000-member church, but you want more; not because you care so much about their souls, but because you want to have the highest number of church members in your state. It makes you feel good and all important.

You have a beautiful wife, but you still want the single sister in the choir. Soon your motivation gravitates away from God and is replaced by things. Yet, the enemy convinces you that you are doing o.k. because you are prospering. Well, the devil trapped you right where he wants you, and you have fallen for it. You better get some prayers going before the storms hit, because all the while he is planning the attack that will destroy you. If your foundation is not the Rock, Christ Jesus Himself, it is sure to crumble.

I cannot emphasize this enough: great Christian music, eloquent speech, and enticing words of man's wisdom have replaced the power that comes through prayer. Pastors and Christian leaders know exactly which button to push to get results. Forget about whether or not they go by it God's way.

Most men of God have acquired the Saul spirit. They are terrified of the people, so they give the people what they want, not what they need. It goes something like this: "If music is what you want, we have it in our church. If it is the message of prosperity, there is plenty of it here. There is healing, too; and you buy it in a prayer cloth. Whatever is convenient for you, we will accommodate. You do not have to pray anymore-just call the prayer line and someone will pray for you. This millennium church is here for your convenience. Just come every Sunday, fill our seats, pay your tithe, provide us with what we need; and we will provide you with what you want. We are well packaged and all around; and if you do not want to come to church on Sunday-just send in your tithes and offering. For your convenience, you can join us on **www.milleniumchurch.com.** See, we accommodate internet members, too!"

What is church coming to? Why is there so much compromise? We are to set the standard for the world, not to adopt its ways. We are to be emulated, not to mimic wrong.

"Having a form of godliness, but denying the power thereof: from such turn away."
II Timothy 3:5

THIS GENERATION LACKS THE ZEAL TO TOUCH HEAVEN AND TO HAVE HEAVEN TOUCH THEM IN RESPONSE

We have replaced the real power of God with sensationalism, hype, and gimmicks. We have trained a generation of people who cannot do exploits for God because they do not know Him. They have not spent enough time with Him to know Him, nor have they listened to Him enough to recognize His voice. This generation does not know anything about spending time in prayer. This generation lacks the zeal to touch heaven, and have heaven touch them in response. We have mentored a generation that does not know how to pray or to wait on God, to lie between the porch and the altar, weeping until deliverance comes.

Oh, no! Men no longer weep. It is deemed a sign of weakness, even if it is before God. We are too composed to cry and too stubborn to bend our knees in prayer. We have passed the job of prayer on to the grandmothers. Thank God for the old mothers of the church whose prayers have sustained some of you until now!

I remember when I got saved a few decades ago. We would go into the woods and the mountains to fast, pray, and wait on God. We learned then how to stay before God in travailing prayer. Those were moments and days that propelled us into our destiny.

WE HAVE PLACED OUR PROPHETS IN DANGER

Today, we have assigned prophets in the church the job to pray, seek God, and bring a word of prophecy for direction. We have put way too much pressure on these poor souls to speak a prophetic word-whether God is speaking or not.

"My sheep hear my voice, and I know them, and they followMe."

John 10:27

We have placed our prophets in danger by substituting their voice for the voice of God. God speaks to us today. God still speaks to His sheep, and His sheep know His voice. Just because you are prospering without prayer, does not mean you are doing the right thing. The devil can also bring prosperity your way.

Remember when Jesus was tempted after his forty-day fast? The devil tried to make a deal with Him that if Jesus would worship him, he would give Him the kingdom, as far as the eyes could see. This is perfect confirmation that all prosperity is not from God. Prosperity is not a sign of spirituality or maturity. This is the very place where Christian men get stuck.

"⁸Again, the devil taketh him up into an exceeding high mountain, and sheweth him all the kingdoms of the world, and the glory of them; 9And saith unto him, All these things will I give then, if thou wilt fall down and worship me. 10Then saith Jesus unto him, Get thee hence, Satan: for it is written, Thou shalt worship the Lord thy God, and him only shalt thou serve."

Matthew 4:8-10

PROSPERITY DOES NOT NECESSARILY MEAN YOU ARE IN THE WILL OF GOD

The devil is still making deals. The devil is asking you to substitute God's way with your own way. You see, when the Spirit of God is upon a man, everyone can see it. When the power of God departs, it leaves so silently, you may not know it. Remember Samson? When Samson lost his power through the deception of Delilah, he did not know that the power had departed. Sad, isn't it? Prosperity does not necessarily mean you are in the will of God if you are not fulfilling the principles of God's word.

"And he awoke from his sleep, and said, 'I will go out as at other times, and shake myself free.' And he did not know that the LORD had left him.

Judges 16:20

His power was so evident, all could see it. Yet when the power departed, it was so subtle even Samson himself did not know it. God's Spirit will not always strive with man. A time comes when He takes leave, and all we are left with is plush organization and material things. God will not always strive for your attention. There comes a time when His Spirit departs, and you may continue to prosper. But, watch out. There is deception lurking in the dark.

He Has You Covered

"12 Wherefore take unto you the whole armor of God, that you may be able to withstand the evil day, and having done all, to stand. 14 Stand therefore, having your loins girt about with truth, and having on the breastplate of righteousness: 15 And your feet shod with the preparation of the gospel of peace; 16 Above all, taking the shield of faith, wherewith ye shall be able to quench all the fiery darts of the wicked. 17 And take the helmet of salvation, and the sword of the Spirit, and watching thereunto with all perseverance and supplication for all saints."

Ephesians 6:13-18

THE DAY YOU GAVE YOUR LIFE TO CHRIST, YOU ENLISTED IN GOD'S ARMY

You are in a battle which started the day you gave your life to Christ. You enlisted in God's army. This army is guaranteed to win, though, if it fights according to the Master's battle plan. There is no other way to do it except by His blueprint (the format laid out in His word). How can you fight personalities without bodies whom you cannot see? Think about it for a while, and you will almost want to give up. But hold on. We are fighting according to the Word of Him Who never fails and Who already won the battle.

God has provided for us a spiritual armor. This armor is invisible to the natural eye, but effective in the spirit realm. The armor is a shroud of defense. The belt of truth, the helmet, the breastplate, and the shield of faith are needed for self defense in this battle. Let us look briefly at their functions.

Belt of Truth: To girt your loins about with truth is to walk in truthfulness, transparency to God and to yourself. It is simply the absence of two-facedness and pretense. The purpose of a belt is to hold in place your clothing. Thus, the truth serves as the base that holds up your armor.

Weapons of Defense

Breastplate of Righteousness: The word "righteousness" means "right standing with God." This kind of righteousness is not acquired. It is imputed upon you by the only righteous One, God Himself, through the Blood of Jesus. There is nothing we can do in our own strength that can make us righteous. For as **Isaiah 64:6** tells us, our righteousness is like filthy rags before God.

How can we stand in righteousness? It is possible only if we come on the basis of the Blood of Jesus. The breastplate covers the chest. Embedded in the chest are some of the most vital organs of the human body, such as the heart and the lungs. The heart is the wellspring of life. Out of the heart flow desires and affections. Even the vilest emotions, such as hatred, spring out of the heart (in this case, the wounded heart).

In **Proverbs 4:23,** we are commanded to keep the heart with all diligence, for out of it springs the issues of life. We have an awesome responsibility to keep our hearts intact. The spiritual breastplate protects the heart, just as the ribs do.

Feet Shod in the Preparation of the Gospel of Peace: To shod your feet with the preparation of the gospel of peace is to put on shoes which are able to send us off in speed preaching the good news. It means to be eager to preach the gospel at all times, in all places, to all men. It means, Man of God, wear your boots for battle. Be prepared. Do not be taken unawares.

Shield of Faith: The shield of faith helps us keep the fiery darts of the enemy at bay. Our faith is our unreserved confidence in God and complete reliance on the truth and integrity of God's word. Fiery darts are flamed-tipped arrows, a barrage of which is released before an assault. They are designed to weaken your defenses.

"Faith comes by hearing, and hearing by the word of God." Build your faith in the Word. You need to eat the Word daily and daily exercise your faith. Remember, without faith, it is impossible to please God.

The Helmet of Salvation: I do not need to tell you how important the head is. You know it. God in His sovereign wisdom encased the human head in the skull. The head contains the brain, the very organ of reason which processes information. The head controls every other part of the body. If your head tells your hand to move, the motion of movement occurs.

Proverbs 23:7 informs us that as a man thinks in his heart so he is. The heart and the mind have a special connection. They work with each other. What controls your mind will influence your heart and ultimately control you life.

The helmet of salvation is designed to protect our mind and our whole perspective towards our Christian faith and life. Evil thoughts and imagination are first conceived in the mind. To put your helmet on is to constantly read, study, and meditate on the Word of God. To "meditate" is to "ponder, mutter, and reflect" on the Word. This is not the meditation as found in eastern religions. That meditation is making your mind draw a blank, which opens your mind up to demonic control. The correct form of meditation is a <u>constant renewal</u> of one's thought patterns and mind sets by the Word of God.

Weapon of Offense-Sword of the Spirit

Apart from having several weapons of defense, we also have one weapon of offense, the SWORD OF THE SPIRIT, which is the Word of God. With this weapon in hand, we need nothing else. This weapon contains the keys to defeat each move of the enemy.

The sword is a thrusting and cutting weapon with a long blade having one or two sharp edges. It is a weapon of offense used to attack an enemy. It is said the best form of defense is to attack. Do not forget that we do not go into this war in our own strength, but by the Spirit of God. The Holy Spirit knows all things and understands all things. He is the Teacher, the One Who leads us into all truths. The Word of God is the Sword of the Spirit. Strength to fight lies in the Spirit's strength in the Word.

JESUS PRAYED AND FOUGHT WITH THE WORD OF GOD

When the devil came against Jesus after his forty-day fast, Jesus fought back with the Sword of the Spirit, the Word of God. Remember, Jesus was the Word, yet He prayed and fought with the Word. Think about this for a minute. I think it is most remarkable. If Jesus prayed the Word, what excuse do we have not to do the same? Why do we think we need to rely only on our own strength for prayer?

The truth is that Jesus needs us to take up His Word and make it our armor and shield. He is the shade upon our right hand. He covers the area that the shield leaves bare. (The shield is usually held in the left hand, leaving the right area of an individual bare.)

THERE IS AN EVIL DAY FOR EACH OF US

Verse thirteen of **Ephesians 6** commands us to be equipped, not with physical or visible armor, but with the armor of the Word so that we can withstand in the evil day, and having done all, to stand. Is this not confirmation that evil and storms come to all of us? There is indeed an evil day for each of us. My evil day may differ from your evil day. <u>The difference between the praying man and the prayer-less man is that one survives the evil day and the other is blown away by the storm.</u>

Watch the life of a man who prays. Regardless of how low he may fall, he always bounces back. His tenacious ability goes way past his own strength. He may lose all his sheep. But, watch out; he is about to rock the world with a new breed of sheep! He may lose his family, as Job did. But his persistence will bring yet another promise of God into fruition.

Inner strength does not simply come because you memorize a verse of scripture and chant it all day long. Inner strength is the result of time spent with God in prayer. In prayer, He breathes into you a fresh breath of life and inspiration that injects into you tenacious and audacious power to live and move in perfect stride, regardless of the situation or circumstances.

This is where we differ from the world. The world watches in awe as we continue in peace and joy, regardless of imminent danger or dire circumstances.

Chapter Three

SUFFERING FROM PWC?- CHANGE YOUR STRATEGY

Are you bugged with the PWC virus of prayerlessness? The devil has located you. He has detected your weakness.

There is an antidote.

The powerful antidote you need always works without fail. It is praying in other tongues. It is indeed a powerful tool in the hands of the believer.

I am not going to debate whether or not speaking in tongues is for today or was a thing of the past. I have experienced the joys of speaking in tongues. I have enjoyed the power embedded in speaking in tongues and a life of consistent prayer because of this gift. Therefore, I encourage you to grab hold of it if you do not already have it and use it if you do have it.

Let us look at the scriptures:

"...praying always with all prayer and supplication in the Spirit, and watching thereunto with all

perseverance and supplication for all saints..."
Ephesians 6:18

PRAYER IS DIFFICULT BECAUSE
IT IS A SPIRITUAL ACT
AND CANNOT BE DONE IN THE FLESH

"Praying always." Are you thinking, "Oh,
that is impossible"? Yet, that is what the Bible
instructs us to do. It seems impossible because we
often pray in our own strength. However, check
out the progression in the scripture: "praying
always...and supplication in THE SPIRIT." It is
hard for us to pray always when we go to God in
our own strength, in our own capacity. The easier
way to pray is to pray in the Holy Ghost praying
in tongues. Prayer is difficult because it is a spiritual act and cannot be done in the flesh if one is to
do it constantly.

**"But ye, beloved, building up yourselves
on your most holy faith, praying in the Holy
Ghost..."**

Jude 1:20

As men, we like to be in charge and in control.
Therefore, praying in the Spirit sometimes does
not appeal to us. It is saying, "I have not clue. I do
not know what to say to you, Lord. I feel silly just
standing here babbling on about what I cannot
understand." Guess what? That is exactly where
God wants you-to totally depend and trust in Him
and His Word.

Prayer generates total dependence on God. Praying in the Spirit is for your benefit. The devil does not have a clue in entirety what God has planned for you or what our innermost desires and thoughts are until you speak them. Speaking in your understanding, therefore, gives the enemy an idea of where you are and what you desire. With such information in his hand, he is able to cause delays and roadblocks. When we pray in the Spirit, we are praying the will and the mysteries of God-which we cannot understand-nor can the devil.

"For he that speaketh in an unknown tongue speaketh not unto men, but unto God: for no man understandeth him; howbeit in the spirit he speaketh mysteries."
I Corinthians 14:2

Speaking in unknown tongues gives you the upper hand. You do not only pray the will of God, you also confuse the devil. How is he going to launch an attack if he is not sure which direction God is taking you? It is for this reason that he frustrates your prayer life. As long as you can stay in prayer, praying the mysteries of God, he loses.

No wonder when you begin to pray, all kinds of things come up unexpectedly to steer you off course. The phone begins to ring, the pager goes off, you abruptly remember something you left incomplete at the office, and the list goes on. Your efforts to pray are being hindered by the enemy attacking your mind. Your mind is a weapon of distraction when you pray. However, you can beat the distraction by praying in the Spirit. And, the additional benefit is that praying in the Spirit is praying the will of God how easy can that be!

THE WILL OF GOD FOR YOUR LIFE IS EMBEDDED IN YOUR PRAYER LANGUAGE

Whenever I am not sure what is the will of God in a situation, I simply pray in tongues and allow time to unfold the mystery of His will. The will of God for you life is securely embedded in your prayer language.

When you pray in tongues, you go past reasoning, arguments of the mind, and spiritual road blocks. It elevates you to the fast track. So, while others are standing in line arguing out their petitions, you have gained easy access.

When you pray in tongues, you pray selflessly and tap into the unlimited resources of God.

When you pray in tongues, you become an instrument and tool in the hands of the Holy Ghost. As you are praying, the Holy Ghost can use you to pray for continents, cities, communities, and churches. It may be He uses you to pray for a pregnant woman in crises, an aircraft in danger in the air, a captain at the mercies of the elements of the sea, someone wrongfully accused in the courts, or someone unknown in imminent danger. Our scope of influence when we pray in the Holy Ghost is limitless.

Prayers offered in tongues travel faster than the speed of light and accomplish much.

You may be asking right now, "How do I speak in another tongue? What do I do to begin this walk in the Spirit?" The following are some scriptures to help you:

"And these signs will accompany those who believe: in My name they will cast out demons; they will speak in new tongues..."

Mark 16: 17

Speaking in tongues is one of the signs that follow the believer. It is not to be rejected but to be embraced. It is a God-given tool that helps you on your Christian journey.

"And they were all filled with the Holy Spirit and began to speak in other tongues, as the Spirit gave them utterance."

Acts 2:4

Speaking in tongues is not an effort of the mind but is given by the assistance of the Holy Spirit dwelling in one.

"And when Paul had laid his hands upon them, the Holy Spirit came on them; and they spoke with tongues and prophesied."

Acts 19:16

The gifts of the Holy Ghost are received by impartation, laying on of hands, or simply by asking God for it.

Let me share a story about a young minister trained in my church. She was brought up as a staunch Catholic, but later gave her life to Christ. At seventeen years old, she joined my church and was rather concerned about speaking in tongues. She felt it was very silly; and, though she embraced most of the teachings, she could not accept the concept of speaking in tongues.

In all-night prayer meetings, a way of life for most of our churches, she would get very frustrated because she covered the prayer topics in less than ten minutes. She did not enjoy praying all night, although she wanted to. She observed that those who prayed in tongues could go on for hours. In her frustration, she went into her prayer closet and asked God to give her the gift of the Spirit-if it really was from Him and of Him.

Days turned into weeks, and nothing happened. One day, as she was praying at home, she just began to speak in tongues. It was so exhilarating for her that she could not stop. To avoid her Catholic parents, who thought praying in tongues to be madness, she would run into the bathroom and stay there as long as she could, just speaking in tongues. (She was concerned that should her parents hear her a trip to the psychiatrist would be enforced).

Fifteen years have passed. She has grown into one of the strongest prayer warriors I know. She also walks in a powerful gift of praise and worship. I cannot believe it is merely coincidence that she walks in power in such a ministry. Prayer is a power producer and strength builder. And this all came about by her simply asking God for the gift.

PRAYING IN THE SPIRIT IS NOT TO SEEK POWER BUT TO SEEK THE FACE OF GOD

Our praying in the Spirit is not to seek power but to seek the face of God. Mighty Man, we need to pray always. I say "we" on purpose. I am not exempt from what I am writing here. This is what we are to do:

We pray when we fill like it, and we pray when we do not.

We pray when we get an immediate answer; and we pray when it feels like God is on vacation.

We pray when we think we know the solution to a problem; and we pray when we cannot find any answers.

We pray when all is well and our children are flourishing like tender olive plaints in our courts; and we pray when our children have gone wayward.

We pray when the wife walks out on us, and we pray when she confesses her undying love for us.

We pray when business is good and we have our money stacked away for a rainy day; and we pray when we are neck-high in debt.

We pray with tears in our eyes, drops of sweat on our brows; and we pray when our hearts are busting with joy unspeakable.

There is no convenient time to pray. We simply pray-always.

WE NEED TO FREE OUR MINDS DAILY FROM THE MISTAKES OF THE PAST

Praying daily means walking in His mercies daily. Mercy means exemption from judgment. We need to free our minds daily from the guilt and mistakes of the past. The mercies of God give us confidence to approach His throne daily. The Blood confirms His mercy, cleans us up, and infuses us with boldness and renewed self-assurance as we go before Him in prayer. I do not know any other way to approach Him except by His Blood.

"22 It is of the LORD's mercies that we are not consumed, because his compassions fail not. 23 They are new very morning: great is thy faithfulness."

Lamentations 3: 22-23

TODAY'S MERCY MAY NOT COVER TOMORROW'S SINS

God releases to us fresh mercies each morning. However, we have to go to Him daily to receive these mercies. How else can we walk consistently in the mercies of God? Today's mercy may not cover tomorrow's sins. We need a constant renewal of His mercy.

I compare the mercies of God to the manna He provided the Children of Israel. The following is what the LORD had commanded:
"16 Gather of it, every man of you, as much as he can eat; you shall take an omer apiece, according to the number of persons whom each of you has in his tent."17 And the people of Israel did so; they gathered, some more, some less. 18 But when they gathered it with an omer, he that gathered much had nothing over, and he that gathered little had not lack; each gathered according to what he could eat. 19 And Moses said to them, "Let no man leave any of it till the morning." 20 But they did not listen to Moses; some left part of it till the morning, and it bred worms and became

35

foul, and Moses was angry with them. 21 Morning by morning they gathered it, each as much as he could eat; but when the sun grew hot; it melted.

Exodus 16:16-21

God provided fresh manna each day-yet some of them felt they had to hold on to some till morning. Is not that just like us? We pray today and think our prayer is enough to take us through the week. And, there are those who do not think they need the mercy of God. The self-righteous man thinks his works are sustaining him.

Upon the wings of each dawn, comes the fresh mercy of God. Those who rise up early to seek it shall find it.

Notice that when the Children of Israel tried to save leftovers for the next day, the food turned to worms. If you try to live off of yesterday's mercy, you are living off worms of the past. As the past goes by, it takes with it its challenges, pains, sins, iniquities, and transgressions. God does not remember yesterday's failures. He puts them in the sea of forgetfulness and extends His mercy yet again.

What He was telling the Children of Israel is, "I am more than enough. You do not need yesterday's provision to sustain you for today. I will give you fresh provision each day. Only ask."

As with the manna, you do not need to save

any leftovers. His mercies are new every morning.

HOLD ON TO THE HORNS OF
THE ALTAR! YOU CANNOT
AFFORD TO FAINT!

Hold on to the horns of the altar. You cannot afford to faint.

"Men ought always to pray, and not to faint"
Luke 18:1

Jesus encouraged his disciples to pray always and not to faint. There is an important ingredient in prayer that is so imperative if we are to receive answers to our prayers. This ingredient is an obstinate adamancy to stay in consistent and prevalent prayer without wavering.

Why was Jesus compelled to exhort us not to faint? Because He was Himself a praying man. He understood the challenges that occur when one embarks on a lifestyle of prayer. Prayer is hard work. Prayer is sweat and blood. Prayer drains you naturally, but renews you spiritually. It is not easy to cultivate a lifestyle of prayer. But it is worth the effort.

Remember, your adversary will do everything and anything in his power to discourage you. The adversary will convince you that God is not interested in your prayers. But, hang in there! God is not only interested, He sends His Holy spirit to pray with you and through you with groanings which cannot be uttered-praying in tongues. Do so, and leave the devil confused about what is going on.

There are many moments in life when "fainting" is a comforting thought. We become weary inside and out from consistent prayer. We can get so discouraged we could fly on the wings of anything that would suggest fainting just a little. Bro, you have got to wake up! The alarm is going off, and the battle is fierce!

You cannot back down or back out.

You cannot break rank, and you cannot throw off your armor.

You cannot come to the battlefield half-dressed. You cannot show up without your helmet.

Please take off your casual shoes, they are not meant for battle. Rather shod your feet with the preparation of the gospel of peace.

You cannot cover your back with the Sword of the Spirit because you are afraid of being exposed about some sin or the other.

Use the Sword of the Spirit for <u>fighting</u>.

Learn how to use your weapons appropriately.

Study to show yourself approved as a worthy soldier.

Come by the Blood, and fight a good fight.

Mix your warfare with faith.

The armor is for defense and the sword is for offense. The Bible never stated anything regarding protection for the back, because you are not meant to turn your back in this battle.

Face your enemy shoulder to shoulder and eyeball to eyeball.

<u>Are you alert yet?</u>

Listen, there is deception out there replacing prayer with human strategy, organization, and systems. I cannot stress enough how much need there is for proper balance.

I love organization. I love and enjoy all the administrative structures that have been put in place by my staff. If there is one thing my staff knows well it is that I always want results. However, underneath the organization and the structures are men and women praying around the clock. The ministry was founded on prayer. We learned early to connect with our

Source, the Founder, the Rock from whence we were hewn.

Through more than twenty-five years in ministry, I cannot begin to tell you the storms that I have had to get through personally; nor can I describe the traumas these storms have brought. The one hundred or more affiliate churches and branches I oversee have all gone through storms. But prayer has kept the weakened knots tied together in the areas that threatened to break. In the process, we have lost some, but gained more.

We have been through character assassination, adverse media exposure, and further storms too many and too diverse to recount by definition. However, we are still prevailing by the cords that bind us strongly to our Source. (If I were to share with you the personal storm and deep anguish I face as I write this book, it would blow your mind.)Nevertheless, I find strength to carry on daily, bearing my cross in prayer as I trudge on this pathway of destiny to fulfill God's mandate for my life.

Therefore, I understand where you may find yourself right now. But, you cannot afford to give up. I am speaking to you as a man. Though many say it is a "man's world," you and I know that we do not always feel that way. Agreed, we have our moments. But, we have our pressures, too. We have been fashioned by society to be "macho." So here we are hiding behind a façade of strength when, indeed, we need help. The help can only be obtained when we go down on our knees and ask for it.

WE CANNOT BUILD A HOUSE FOR GOD IN WHICH HE WILL NEVER LIVE

We need to set our properties right. We cannot build a house for God in which He will never live because we never created an atmosphere to keep Him there. We can create an atmosphere for Him to visit through our praise and worship. But will God call your structure a home for Him where He can come and abide with you always?

The same goes for the man who is building a business, his home, or his career in his own strength. Apparently, he does not need God until calamity strikes. Then prayer becomes all so important. Wake up! You need a fresh connection to your power base. "For you strength is but only a little." Your ability to make it on the stock market is not security. (Consider what would happen should the stock market crumble.)

"Except the LORD build the house, they labor in vain that built it, except the LORD keep the city, the watchman wakes but in vain."

Psalm 127:1

As Christian men, we should be clear about who is our Source. As heads, we need to acknowledge and put in proper place the Head of our life. He is priority and nothing else. Confuse your priority, and you mess up your structure.

There is a Master Builder Who is willing to work with you until your purpose is through. He will not force you to rely on Him, but He is encouraging you to. Prayer is taking your eyes off yourself, your circumstances and social status, and looking unto God in humility and total dependence.

Chapter Four

HINDRANCES OF A FAST PACED SOCIETY WORSEN THE EPIDEMIC

The hustle and bustle of our world today is unbelievable. Everything is fast-paced, and we have a quick fix for everything. The information/computer age has increased the pace of life-more than a notch. There is no broken gadget that super glue cannot fix. Manual labor has been replaced with the touch of a button. Everything can happen as and when you want it-fast! Anything that requires waiting is a "pressure task," and it so irritates us. Even our kids have no time to stop and breathe. Society has robbed our future leaders of the very virtue of patience.

Spending time with God can sometimes be a daunting task, if not altogether impossible, in light of our daily schedules. As the phone rings, the pager goes off, the laptop is filled with e-mail messages, the fax machine rolls out even more messages, God gets left out in between the "to-do list" and the pressing errands that spring up so easily as our day progresses.

Take a deep breath. Slow down. There is a

stop sign ahead-a waiting period until the light is green. Impatience will not work well if you are going to take up your God-given responsibility of praying ceaselessly.

I will share another story with you that may seem funny, but is true:

My older daughter was recently going through a tough period in her life, as many young adults do. As a graduate student, out there on her own, she was often faced with tough decisions and choices that she knew would alter the course of her life. She was faced with a particularly tough situation and needed a quick fix from God. As the pressure mounted, God seemed ever so silent.

One evening my daughter went to a Chinese restaurant with her friends. As they ate dinner, a thought came to her-God could speak to her through a fortune cookie! She quickly grabbed one from the table to see what the Lord had to say to her. Guess what the fortune cookie said? "You need to be patient"-the exact words of advice I gave her when she shared her challenges with me.

She had enough training in the Word to know that one needs to wait on God when in doubt. But the pressure sent her searching for the Word of God in the wrong place.

What is the pressure of waiting doing to you? Are you calling the "Psychic Hotline," when no one is looking, in hopes that the Lord will give you a word? Watch out! You are walking in the devil's territory.

Is the pressure of waiting for a Godly spouse so severe that sex on the internet has become your source of release? Perhaps your wife has become like the contentious woman Proverbs describes, who nags from morning until night; and now you have found a new way of escape-on the "roof top." However, in this particular episode, you are not alone on that roof top. (You live there on the roof top with another contention waiting to happen!)

When the pressures of life strike, what is your source of release? How do you face the issues for which you have neither solutions nor answers?

Do you seek out the prophets in the land and try to twist God's arm for a word, or do you simply thrust yourself in His everlasting arms?

THERE IS A WORD THAT COMES TO THOSE WHO WAIT ON GOD

There is a word that comes to those who wait on God. He may not give you the solution out of your problem. He may simply give you enough strength to pull through until He is ready to unveil the mystery of His will.

Don't we just hate it when we do not know

what to do? Sometimes we feel beaten and vulnerable when we are faced with the strange hurricanes and tornadoes of life. We give everyone the impression that we know what we are doing; when, sometimes, they can clearly see we are indeed lost and need help.

GOD IS NOT IMPRESSED WITH YOUR STRENGTH, HE IS TOUCHED BY YOUR VULNERABILTY

Men, this cover-up work is killing us. God is not impressed with your strength. He is touched by your vulnerability. STOP, take a minute and regroup.

What is so difficult about admitting your weakness to God? He is a loving Father. Like with me, you may not have experienced the love and protection of your natural father as a child. Do not close the door to God for He is unlike your natural father. He will never leave you nor forsake you, and your weakness only gives Him an opportunity to show off His strength.

Chapter Five

THE PRIDE OF LIFE

This is a bitter pill to swallow. Pride is in our way, and we need to be aware and swallow the only pill that can help us heal from its symptoms.

Weigh this: Could it be that PRIDE is what is keeping us from bowing our knees and admitting our need for God? We need God not only for the weighty decisions of our lives, careers, and businesses; but we need Him also for the very ostensibly small ones.

"If my people, which are called by My name shall humble themselves and pray, and seek My face, and turn from their wicked ways; then will I hear from heaven, and will forgive their sin, and will heal their land."
II Chronicles 7:14

Watch this: **"If my people...shall humble themselves."** The antonym for **"humble"** is **"arrogance,"** and the synonym for **"arrogance"** is "pride."

God is saying, **"Here is the deal."** You are My people, and you are called by no other name but Mine. I will make a deal with you that if you humble yourself and pray, (watch the progression), and seek My face and turn from your wicked ways, I will cut you some slack and hear you. I will forgive you and heal your land."

Your land may be your home, your church, your business, etc. God is saying, "I see you struggle, mighty man. I want to reach out and help you. But you haven't stopped to invite me. You're acting like you have it all under control. But, son, I feel your need tugging at me. I see pride also. You're not able to ask for help. I know exactly where you are. I understand and have a solution and a plan for you. But, can you just trust Me?"

He is saying, "Take a moment, son, and let's be real. Take the mask off and shed off the scales of falsehood, and let's have an honest conversation. I know that the sin of pride has kept us apart, but it's okay. Come, level with Me now, and seek My face. In other words, search for Me diligently. You know I cannot behold iniquity. So repent of your sins, and I will step right in and bring healing."

THE TOXIN OF PRIDE IS A KILLER

The toxin of pride is a killer. The sin of pride is abhorrent to God. Put it this way-God simply can't stand it!

"...And he shall spread forth his hands in the midst of them, as he that swimmeth spreadeth forth his hands to swim: and he shall bring down their pride together with the spoils of their hands."

Isaiah 25:11

"And I will break the pride of your power; and I will make your heaven as iron, and your earth as brass"

Leviticus 26: 19

What is pride? Pride is self-importance and self-centeredness, and an unduly high opinion of one's self worth. Pride causes one to see the world only through his/her own eyes. Any other opinion is inferior to the prideful man. Pride says, "Look at me. I am high and lifted up. I don't need you. I have all that I need, and that is myself."

Egocentricity is knocking us off God's favor list. God cannot stand pride! It does not matter if it is the pride of a nation or the pride of an individual, God will make sure that pride comes down. Think about instances where mankind thought they were untouchable because of some creation of their own hand-for example, the "unsinkable" Titanic. In April, 1912, nature tragically proved man wrong about that one.

PRIDE COMES IN AS OUR NEED FOR OUR CREATOR DECREASES

Pride comes in as our need for our Creator decreases. The created says to its Creator, "I don't need You. I will do fine on my own." How presumptuous is that? The Creator has the blue print. He knows exactly what His creation needs and when His created needs it.

"The wicked, through the pride of his

countenance, will not seek after God: God is not in all his thoughts"

Psalms 10:4

The car manufacturer makes the car in such a way that servicing is needed every three months for smooth riding of the car. "The car that argues" with the manufacturer that it does not need any servicing will soon break down. It is just a natural law.

When a man decides that he will never eat again, he is sure to be buried rather close to the date of his decision. Whether he eats or not does not change the fact that his body needs food to survive.

GOD MAKES IT HIS BUSINESS TO BRING DOWN THE PRIDEFUL MAN

God makes it His business to bring down the prideful man. I have seen many young Christian men miss it in life because they thought they had it all together. When you have it altogether you do not need God, or anybody else.

Let's go back to the roots of pride. Pride was first recorded when Lucifer thought it would be a really neat idea to be like God. In other words, he did not need God. His self-centeredness told him he could make it on his own, that he could be compared to God, and thus he could usurp God's throne. Lucifer had recognition, a prestigious position, and beauty-which all added up to POWER.

The true character of a man is seen when he is placed in power. Power in the hands of man is like a blood sucking leech on flesh. It just cannot get enough.

Lucifer had talent. This guy could sing! He was beautiful and powerful. Seeming prosperity was soon to test him-

"For the turning away of the simple shall slay them, and the prosperity of fools shall destroy them."
Proverbs 1:32

The prestige got to Lucifer's head, and he thought "he was IT."

If you want to test a man for pride, just place him in the midst of wealth. How does he treat people? How does he treat his father, his family, and his peers? I have watched many young men, who have come into prestige and prosperity, change adversely. I have seen many try to buy their way to the top. However, the book of Psalms clearly tells us that promotion comes from God.

Pride can be hidden safely in the life of a "poor" man, but prosperity exposes it. We have been created with a perpetual need for our Creator. Pride will deny you the joys and comfort of God's guidance and leadership. The pride of life is a self-destruct mechanism. It will place you in opposition to your Creator and in battle with yourself. In either situation, you cannot win.

PRIDE IS THE QUICKEST WAY OF DESCENT

In our Christian journey, pride is the quickest way of descent. Nebuchadnezzar was man filled with pride. He commanded kingdoms and nations and was a force and power to reckon with in his day. He commanded thrones and dominions. When his pride got in the way, he became an example for God to show us clearly and distinctively what pride can do to a man.

God turned the high-mindedness of Nebuchadnezzar into foolishness and sent him on his way, mad.

"**30 The king spake, and said is not this great Babylon, that I have built for the house of the kingdom by the might of my power, and for the honour of my majesty?'**

31 While the word was in the king's mouth, there fell a voice from heaven, saying, O king Nebuchadnezzar, to thee it is spoken; The kingdom is departed thee. 32 And they shall drive them from men, and thy dwelling shall be with the beasts of the field: they shall make thee to eat grass as oxen, and seven times shall pass over thee, until thou know that the most High ruleth in the kingdom of men and giveth it to whomsoever he will. 33 The same hour was the thing fulfilled upon Nebuchadnezzar: and he was driven from**

men, and did eat grass as an oxen, and his body was wet with the dew of heaven, till his hairs were grown like eagles' feathers, and his nails like birds' claws.

34 And at the end of the days I Nebuchadnezzar lifted up mine eyes unto heaven, and mine understanding returned unto me, and I blessed the most High, and I praised and honoured him that liveth for ever, whose dominion is an everlasting dominion, and his kingdom is from generation to generation: 35 And all the inhabitants of the earth are reputed as nothing and he doeth according to his will in the army of heaven, and among the inhabitants of the earth: and none can stay his hand, or say unto him, What does thou?

36 At the same time my reason returned unto me; and for the glory of my kingdom, mine honour and brightness returned unto me; and my counselors and my lords sought unto me; and I was established in my kingdom, and excellent majesty was added unto me. 37 Now I Nebuchadnezzar praise and extol and honour the King of heaven, all whose works are truth, and his ways judgment: and those that walk in PRIDE he is able to abase."

Daniel 4:30-37

Can this be any clearer? What I like most about these scriptures is that he lived to tell his own story. No one wrote it for him. He wrote it in his own words. He remembered the time when he went insane. He remembered the details of his insanity and his inability to restore himself. Can you imagine what torment that must have been-to be trapped inside a barricade of insanity and have enough sense to be aware of it-to know you are losing it, and yet have no power to control yourself?

Nebuchadnezzar ends with words of praise to the only wise and living God, Who sits in the circles of the earth. And he ends with a factual word of caution to those who walk in pride-know that God is able to subjugate.

I feel the need to provide you more scriptures because of the seriousness of this virus call pride.

PRIDE IS AN ABOMINATION TO GOD

To point out the consequences of walking in pride, nothing and no one says it better than the following scripture.

"Every one that is proud in heart is an abomination to the LORD: though hand join in hand, he shall not be unpunished."
Proverbs 16:5

If I were to tell you that pride is an abomination, you would likely say I was taking things too far. But the Bible says that clearly in Proverbs 16:5. "Abomination" is another word for "atrocity, eyesore, hatred, or outrage. "Pretty intense, isn't itCan you feel the heart of the Father towards pride?

THE ANTIDOTE TO BREAKING PRIDE
IS PRAYER AND FASTING

The antidote to breaking pride is prayer and fasting.

"He that is of a proud heart stirreth up strife: but he that putteth his trust in the LORD shall be made fat."
Proverbs 28:25

The proud heart, because of its stubbornness, stirs up strife-because pride wants its way always and is always right in its own eyes. It inevitably produces strife wherever it is found. No one man is exempt from pride. It is subtle and can fall in the lap of anyone who is making progress in life. It can gradually eliminate your need for God.

Sometimes systems and organizations eliminate your need for God. Why ask God for money if you can use your credit card? Why believe Him to pay off your house when you can get a thirty-year mortgage? Society with all its great technology is steering us away from the only sure foundation we have-God.

As men, we have to work hard at killing pride. Society accepts it and almost expects it from us. But, we need to be careful. Pride will lead us to a fall. Placing yourself on your knees daily is a deterrent to pride. A man on his knees is a man in need of his Maker. Honor and humility are inseparable as are pride and fall.

"Pride goeth before destruction, and a haughty spirit before a fall."

Proverbs 16:18

"A man's pride shall bring him low: but honour shall uphold the humble in spirit.

Proverbs 29:23

Pride releases the wrath of the Lord, and humility releases His favor. It is indeed a fearful thing to fall into the hand of the Lord. I will opt for His mercy anytime.

Rushing? STOP and take a moment. Take a deep breath. Are you struggling with the act of prayer? Check yourself. Pride may be separating you from God. Repent and move on to another level. I encourage you to search your heart briefly before reading the next chapter-it will release your heart and bring liberty to your soul.

Chapter Six

WHATEVER EVER WILL BE?A POOR CASE OF ILLUSION

"The effectual fervent prayer of a righteous man availeth much."

James 5:16

There are many Christians out there who do not think that prayer is really for them. They think that one must be gifted in the area of prayer or called specifically in the prayer ministry to pray consistently. That is a lie.

Prayer is for everyone. Some are of the attitude that if God is God and knows the end from the beginning, and vice versa, then God will work things out in His own time. I have heard many Christians say, "God gave me a word of prophecy and that settles it. I will just wait for it to come to pass." By waiting, they never pray the word into fruition. They never remind God of this word of prophecy. They never war with the word of prophecy. They simply daydream about it.

WE MUST ENFORCE GOD'S PROPHETIC WORD

You need to enforce God's prophetic word and

superimpose the victory into this realm. For example:
The policeman is the law-enforcing agent of the
government. He ensures that the law is obeyed and
carried out. The sight of an officer in uniform is
enough to bring order into certain chaotic
situations. When he pulls out his badge, he
confirms his authority (confirming that he has the
backing of the government and the support of
other law enforcement workers). When he pulls
out his gun, he is telling you he has the power.

Let us consider the prophetic word of God
or, indeed, His written Word as the law. We are
His law-enforcing agents. He has given us His son
Jesus as the badge of authority. He has given His
Word (the gun) as the very source of power. You
take that word, and you enforce it. You arrest
every contrary spirit that seeks to steal, delay, or
kill the word of God. You act as the law enforcing
agent for the word.

Do not forget that the devil comes to steal,
kill, and destroy. You and the word are his target.

Come with me for a while, and let us break
bread. I want this book to be as simple as can it can
be, so we do not miss the message and the mandate
of God for us to pray always.

**"18 This charge I commit unto thee, son
Timothy, according to the prophecies which went
forth on thee, that thou by them mightest war a
good warfare; 19 holding faith, and a good**

conscience; which some having put away concerning faith have made shipwreck."

I Timothy 1:18 & 19

By this charge, Paul gave Timothy the keys whereby he would be able to secure the purposes of God concerning his life and would not end up shipwrecked in the great spiritual battle raging in the heavenlies and on earth. He also made it clear that the manifestation of God's promises and the prophecies would be brought about by warfare.

THE GREAT DECEPTION
FROM THE FORCES OF DARKNESS

Years in ministry have brought to my attention the great deception from the forces of darkness is that "as long as God has given the promise of prophecy it will come to pass. So just relax, sleep, and wait for fulfillment."

With hindsight, do you not realize that the greatest battles you ever faced in your life came soon after a strong prophetic word from God? Maybe it was a rhema word God gave you in your personal time of fellowship. Yet everything contrary to the word took place.

Let me establish this simple truth. Apart from the written word, the devil does not know the exact purposes of God for your life in a particular area until God reveals it through prophecy. As soon as the devil and his troops hear of this word of prophecy, they take measures in the realm of the spirit and in the realms of the natural to ensure it never comes to pass.

When the devil puts up a fight for the word of God, things get worse before they get better. They only get better when we hang in there in faith. We doubt too quickly and give up too easily. We run from the battle in doubt and defeat.

Must we be reminded of Esther, a woman who was willing to believe God to step into a situation at the expense of her own life? Stop doubting the word of God when things seem to be going the wrong direction. It is just a demonic onslaught to take you off course. Stay on course, do not give in to pain, keep pushing and keep persisting until something breaks. Ignorance of what the devil is doing will send you packing and walking away from your purpose.

WE ARE CALLED TO WAR FOR THE PROPHECIES OF GOD

Why on earth would Paul, the same Paul who once killed the believers, now saved by grace, tell Timothy to war with the prophecies? Perhaps Timothy had a nonchalant attitude toward the prophesies of God, and that bothered Paul. Paul may have said to himself, "Timothy is too 'cool' about this prophecy. He needs to wake up in prayer, or the prophecy will never come to pass." Perhaps Timothy was too intact and too composed to show any distress about the delay of the word of God.

"Therefore my people are gone into captivity, because they have no knowledge."

Isaiah 5:13

"Lest Satan should get an advantage of us; for we are not ignorant of his devices."

II Corinthians 2:11

The devil throws a party when he comes into contact with an ignorant believer. He draws a circle around him because the believer lacks understanding of the principles of the kingdom and the rules of battle in the realm of the spirit.

THE LORD HAS THOUSANDS OF PROMISES WAITING TO BE MANIFESTED IN THE LIVES OF BELIEVERS

Maybe you are thinking, "I haven't received any prophetic word from the LORD over my life." Hear this. God has thousands of promises in the Bible waiting to be manifested in the lives of believers. Most of these promises do not come to pass because we do not want to pay the price to effect their manifestation.

You may know the story of Daniel. If you do not, please take a few minutes to read Daniel 10:1-14. In this account, we see Daniel on a twen-ty-one-day fast, seeking some words from God pertaining to things that would befall His people in the future. At the end of the third week, Daniel is by the great river Hiddekel (otherwise known as the Tigris in these modern times and now flowing in the nation of Iraq).

By the banks of the river, Daniel beholds the most terrible sight-that of an angel coming right out of spiritual warfare with the ruling satanic prince over the Persian Empire. So savage has been the fight in the heavens over Persia that the angel is described as having a face that resembled lightening, eyes that blazed like lamps of fire, and arms and feet like that of colored brass.

This will give you an idea of how fierce battles in the spirit can be when we engage in combat with the forces of darkness. For Daniel, the sight was so terrible to behold, he fainted! After his resuscitation, the angel told him a crucial fact and revelation of what caused the delay of Daniel's answer to his prayer.

"But the prince of the kingdom of Persia withstood me one and twenty days; but, lo, Michael, one of the chief princes came to help me; and I remained there with the kings of Persia."
Daniel 10:13

On the way from heaven with an answer to prayer, the angel encountered the evil prince of Persia. A territorial principality that governed the whole Persian Empire interrupted the angel, trying to stop him from reaching Daniel with the message from God. In the mean time, Daniel was on his face in PERSISTANT PRAYER.

He did not give up the fight and take a nap. He was desperate enough to be consistent, simply obeying God's principle of praying without ceasing. There is reward that comes when one persists in prayer. There is victory that existed before the fight which is released into the natural realm when we stay consistent.

Mighty Man, I am telling you we win! We win if we stick to the word, the plan, the way-which is not by any means easy, but effective. Do not think for one moment your prayers do not touch God, because they do.

"4 (For the weapons of our warfare are not carnal, but mighty through God to the pulling down of strong holds;) 5 Casting down imaginations, and every high thing that exalteth itself against the knowledge of God, and bringing into captivity every thought to the obedience of Christ;"

II Corinthians 10:4-5

Let me end this chapter with a couple more of my personal stories.

I was scheduled to be on a flight to a neighboring African country a few years ago. Preparations had been made for my arrival and speaking engagements and advertisements had gone out. Now when it came time for me to travel, the Lord told me specifically not to go on the flight. Many of my people had worked hard to put things in place for my arrival. However, I reluctantly called and canceled. To make a long story short, the flight I was supposed to be on crashed.

Another time I was visiting one of my friends in the ministry in the Virgin Islands when CNN issued a tornado warning approaching the Island. The church and the pastor I had visited were greatly disturbed. Of course, I was also concerned since I was on the island at the time. I asked the Lord what to do, and He told me to speak to the storm and command it to go back to where it had come from. I prayed just as the Lord commanded.

The storm kept approaching as we listened in for updates. When it hit the shores of the island, however, it made a U-turn and went back in the direction it had come. Tell me that prayer does not change things!

Years later I visited the same island; and one night, as I slept, the Lord woke me up and asked me to leave town immediately. It was almost midnight. I called the airlines to check if they had any flights out, and I was told there were no flights at that time of the night.

I then told my assistant with whom I was

traveling to catch a taxi to the airport and find us a flight out of there, while I went ahead and packed my things. He looked at me as though I was mad. His response was that there were no flights at that time of the night. I told him simply to do as I had told him. He unenthusiastically did as I had asked. He called me later to confirm that there were no flights leaving the island. I insisted he check again. He called back a few minutes later to say that an American Airlines flight scheduled to leave in the morning had decided to leave the island at about 1:00 A.M.

We made it off the island, and the storm hit not long after we left. There is power in prayer and constant communication with our Maker. When we are in relationship with God, He speaks to us; and we recognize His voice because we are familiar with it.

Chapter Seven

THE PILLS THAT WORKED IN THE PAST STILL CURE PWC

PRAYING MEN OF THE BIBLE

There are endless accounts of men in the Bible who prayed through the promises of God.

Elijah was such a man, who prayed that it would not rain for three and a half years. And, for that exact number of years, the rains did not come down. Whey he prayed again that it should rain, rain poured out of heaven:

"And he prayed again, and the heaven gave rain, and the earth brought forth her fruit."

James 5:18

Elijah's capacity to persist in prayer makes him a man to imitate.

Daniel was also a man of prayer whose prayers reached heaven, brought into manifestation the prophecies of God for a whole nation, and exalted God in a Godless society. Daniel's boldness was evident. His prayers kept him secure in a society where serving God was a suicidal attempt. He was willing to die for what he believed in rather than bow to man. In Daniel, we find a man consistent in prayer and bold in his beliefs.

There is the story of David, whose relationship with God and prayers brought about the majority of the Psalms we enjoy today. David's dependence on God cannot be missed. David was a man of prayer, praise, and worship.

Moses was a man who interceded constantly for the people of Israel. He was a leader upon whom the people depended greatly. He was aware that he could not lead the people of God other than by the divine direction of God. Thus, he always asked God what to do next and in which direction to go.

The pressure on Moses must have been daunting. He had the responsibility of leading a whole nation out of bondage without knowing the details of God's plan. He had to believe God each day for new direction, because of a murmuring people whose attitude led him back to his knees seeking God's face. His character and innate neediness for God awarded him the title, "meekest man on the face of the earth." Yet, even so, the one time pride got in the way, he missed seeing the promise land. (The story of Moses can be found in Exodus).

Abraham, father of all nations, was a man of

faith and prayer. He held on to God's impossible promise until the manifestation. Today, you and I are heirs of that promise.

The praying men of the Bible enjoyed remarkable promises because of their relationship with God based on prayer. The number of them is countless. I share only a few to establish the fact that we can do greater works than those who came before us.

The prayer life of one who touches me the most is Cornelius, a man who was introduced to us simply as a "certain man." The only identity we have for this man is that he was a centurion, who belonged to an Italian band. This man has no genealogical background significantly linking him to anyone or any group of people. Cornelius, however, by-passed all those who had favorable possibility of being mentioned in the Bible and, through his prayer life, secured for himself a position in Biblical accounting. He was not even what we would term a believer. Yet his heart for God and his prayers did not go unnoticed:

"There was a certain man in Caesarea called Cornelius, a centurion of the band called the Italian band, 2 A devout man, and one that feared God with all his house, which gave much alms to the people, and prayed to God alway. 3 He saw in a vision evidently about the ninth hour of the day an angel of God coming in to him, and saying unto him, Cornelius. 4 And when he

**looked on him, he was afraid, and said, what is it,
Lord? And he said unto him, Thy prayers and
thine alms are come up The Pills That Worked in
the Past for a memorial before God. 5 And now send
men to Joppa, and call for one Simon, whose
surname is Peter:"**

Acts 10:1-6

The scripture says he prayed always. His
continuity touched the heart of God, and God had
no choice by to intercede and send him the help he
needed.

PRAYER BREAKS ALL LIMITS

Prayer breaks all limits. If an unbeliever can
reach God through relentless prayers, what can
you do? Time and space do not allow me to write
about the detailed accomplishment of other men of
prayer-as Job, Paul, and many more. But understand
that all these men are just like you and me.

The foundation of the early church was
prayer. After the ascension of Jesus, the disciples
continued with the work He had started. They had
been with Jesus long enough to adopt His ways.
They knew that prayer was what saw Him through
to the end. We find them praying together countless
times. The foundation of the church was nothing
but prayer. Prayer brought unity, and unity in
prayer produced the power of God.

**"These all continued with one accord in
prayer and supplication, with the women, and Mary**

the mother of Jesus, and with his brethren."

Acts 1:14

"And they continued stedfastly in the apostles' doctrine and fellowship, and in breaking of bread, and in prayers."

Acts 2:42

THE FIRST CHURCH HAD BALANCE

The first church had balance. They had their doctrines for sure, but they learned to balance their doctrine with prayer. Prayer was the base for everything they did, including their decisions.

"And they prayed, and said, Thou, Lord, which knowest the hearts of all men, shew whether of these two thou has chosen,"

Acts 3:1

Pentecost happened as a result of prayer:

"And when they had prayed, the place was shaken where they were assembled together; and they were all filled with the Holy Ghost, and they spake the word of God with boldness."

Acts 4:31

The following few scriptures are about men of God who continued in prayer and how they encouraged the church to pray. Read them carefully. You will find they are helpful. If will help open the eyes of your understanding. Paul, the writer of most of the Epistles, had a consistent prayer life.

70

He also encouraged the church to pray always.

"For this cause we also, since the day we heard it, do not cease to pray for you, and to desire that ye might be filled with the knowledge of his will in all wisdom and spiritual understanding:"

Colossians 1:9

"Continue in prayer; and watch in the same with thanksgiving;"

Colossians 4:2

"Withal praying also for us, that God would open unto us a door of utterance, to speak the mystery of Christ, for which I am also in bonds:"

Colossians 4:3

"We give thanks to God always for you all, making mention of you in our prayers;"

I Thessalonians 1:2

"Night and day praying exceedingly that we might see your face, and might perfect that which is lacking in your faith"

I Thessalonians 3:10

"Now Peter and John went up together into the temple at the hour of prayer, being the ninth hour."

Acts 3:1

"But we will give ourselves continually to prayer, and to the ministry of the word."

Acts 6:4

"Epaphras, who is one of you, a servant of Christ, saluteth you, always labouring fervently for you in prayers, that ye may stand perfect and complete in all the will of God."

Colossians 4:12

Pray without ceasing."

I Thessalonians 5:17

"Finally, brethren, pray for us, that the word of the Lord may have free course, and be glorified, even as it is with you:"

I Thessalonians 3:1

"I exhort therefore, that, first of all, supplications, prayers, intercessions, and giving of thanks, be made for all men:"

I Timothy 2:1

"I will therefore that men pray every where, lifting up holy hands, without wrath and doubting."

I Timothy 2:8

"Is any among you afflicted? Let him pray. Is any merry? Let him sing psalms."

James 5:13

"Peter therefore was kept in prison: but prayer was made without ceasing of the church onto God for him."

Acts 12:5

"And when they had ordained them elders in every church, and had prayed with fasting, they commended them to the Lord, on whom they believed."

Acts 14:23

The early church lived a life of prayer. They survived the times because they prayed. If the church of today would survive the times, then prayer has to go forth-prayer for the nations, prayer for the communities, prayer for the saved, prayer for the unsaved. Prayer for the sick, prayer for the afflicted, prayer for all saints, prayer for presidents and rulers of our world today are all our call to duty.

However, you need to grow in prayer. You need to start by praying for yourself and building your way up to heavy-duty stuff. Study the Word and arm yourself with the power of the sword and take your position.

Chapter Eight

THE ULTIMATE PRAYER MAN

There is a man that I admire greatly whose prayer life I urge you to emulate. He lived a rather short life and his ministry was even shorter. Yet the impact He made is still felt in our world today. His life has transformed the hearts of many a stubborn man and delivered the captives from the prisons that once held them bound.

Songs are still sung about Him, and no force or power has been able to erase His name or His influence from the world. This ultimate Man of Prayer about whom I am writing is none other than Christ Jesus, our Lord.

He performed many miracles and walked on water. He raised the dead and healed the sick. The Bible clearly tells us that He was all man.

He was subject to temptations just as we are, and yet He was without sin. We want to pass Him off as the Son of God, so... .Yes, He was the Son of God. But never make light of the fact that He was just like you and me. We often do not consider that He experienced exactly the same experiences we face. We look to other persons in the Bible for understanding of a way to walk through troubles (mind you, there is nothing wrong in that) and dismiss Jesus from our consideration because He was God and somehow above the human experience.

Remember that He was indeed a man, and thereby touched by the feelings of your infirmities. He understands and knows your weaknesses and your frailty. That is why He is forever making intercession for you.

Do not tell me He did not feel what you feel. Remember Isaiah's account of Him? He was bruised for our iniquity. He was wounded for our transgressions. The chastisement of our peace was laid upon Him. He was reprimanded for your sins. He took your place and took your punishment. He was a man of sorrows, well acquainted with grief, despised and rejected. Tell me He does not understand what you are going through?

We often think that Jesus performed miracles because He was God. I am here to tell you, though God/Man, Jesus performed the miracles BECAUSE HE PRAYED. He was securely connected. As a man, His only way of contacting the Father was through prayer. Jesus often retreated into the mountains by Himself to pray. Before every major decision or miracle, we find that Jesus was away somewhere praying.

JESUS FASTED AND PRAYED BEFORE EMBARKING ON HIS MINISTRY

Before Jesus stepped out in ministry, He

fasted and prayed in the wilderness for forty days and nights. He did not just wake up one morning and say, "Hmm, I feel good today. I'm excited about God so let me start a ministry." No, He spent time before God, waiting in fasting and prayers.

JESUS PRAYED BEFORE SELECTING THE TWELVE

"12 And it came to pass in those days, that he went out into a mountain to pray, and continued all night in prayer to God. 13 And when it was day, he called unto him his disciples: and of them he chose twelve, whom also he named apostles;"

Luke 6:12-13

Before Jesus chose the twelve disciples, He went off into the mountain to pray all night. He could not choose the twelve by sight. He had to choose them through the Father's eye-for each of these disciples had a purpose to fulfill, even Judas.

Today, as we embark into business, we seldom pray to God for guidance. We select a partner logically and carry on our business in the flesh. God is interested in everything that we do. With the correct choices, we will ultimately fulfill God's will through us. Peter's purpose had to be fulfilled, but that would not have happened if Jesus did not seek the Father before making His choice. If you are to succeed in life, you need to ask

God to bring your way people whose lives you will affect and who will also positively affect you. Within this Divine order, in the end, the will of the Father will be fulfilled in your life as well as in theirs. How do you choose your board members? Do you just select those who look good, or do you ask God's opinion because only He sees and knows the hearts of men?

JESUS CONTINUED TO PRAY WHILE IN MINISTRY

"And in the morning, rising up a great while before day, he went out, and departed into a solitary place, and there prayed."

Mark 1:35

As Jesus embarked on His ministry, we find Him praying to the Father several times in solitude. His source of power can be traced directly to what He did in His quiet time. What do you do in your quiet time? Are you surfing the web, or are you seeking God's face. Are you looking at the statistics which always point you to your limitations? Jesus' dependence on God the Father was apparent. In Mark 1:35, we find Him rising up a great time before the day begins to pray.

"And it came to pass, that, as he was alone praying, his disciples were with him:"

Luke 9:18

"And it came to pass, that, as he was praying in a certain place, when he ceased, one of his

disciples said unto him, Lord, teach us to pray, as John also taught his disciples."

Luke 11:1

JESUS PRAYED BEFORE MAJOR MIRACLES

Preceding most of Jesus' supernatural encounters, we find Him praying.

" 23 And when he had sent the multitudes away, he went up into a mountain apart to pray: and when the evening was come, he was there alone. 24 But the ship was now in the midst of the sea, tossed with waves: for the wind was contrary. 25 And in the fourth watch of the night Jesus went unto them, walking on the sea. 26 And when the disciples saw him walking on the sea, they were troubled, saying it is a spirit; and they cried out for fear."

Matthew 14:23-26

Many of us think that Jesus just decided to walk on the water to prove a point-that He was God/Man. However, read the above scripture carefully. Jesus went out to pray. He prayed until the fourth watch. A "watch" constitutes of three hours. Therefore, if Jesus prayed until "the fourth watch," then I suggest to you that He prayed for twelve hours. His supernatural ability to walk on water occurred because of prayer. Do not take this prayer thing for granted! Prayer is powerful.

"...he took Peter and John and James, and went up into a mountain to pray. And as he prayed,

the fashion of his countenance was altered, and his raiment was white and glistering."

Luke 9:28, 29

This was the time of His Transfiguration. Notice He had gone up to the mountain to pray with three of His disciples. Luke tells us that, as He prayed, His appearance changed. Do you see the potency of prayer? Do you feel the power of prayer? Prayer places you outside the natural realm with its limitations into a realm of impossibilities. Prayer coupled with faith is dynamite! It releases God's hand for miracles, signs, and wonders. Jesus assured us that if we walk in the ways of God, greater works than He did we shall do.

THE FEWER THE INTERRUPTIONS FOR PRAYER THE BETTER THE FOCUS AND INTENSITY

An important thing to notice in most of the scriptures above is the fact that Jesus always went into seclusion to pray. The fewer interruptions and hindrances you have in prayer, the better the focus and intensity. Praying in the early hours of the morning, when most of the world is sleeping, is definitely a way to reduce mental interruptions and natural ones as well. In the early hours of morning, the mind is less taxed. I greatly encourage you to find your own quiet time in a day to spend with God. The great men of our recent past were able to obtain outstanding victories through the avenue of persistent prayer. John Knox and Smith

Wigglesworth, to name two for example, made great impact on their generation solely because they were men of prayer.

JESUS PRAYED HIMSELF THROUGH THE CROSS EXPERIENCE

"Then cometh Jesus with them unto a place called Gethsemane, and saith unto the disciples, Sit ye here, while I go and pray yonder."
Matthew 26:36

The most touching and intense prayer time Jesus had, in my opinion, were the hours before His death in the Garden of Gethsemane as His flesh and Spirit battled with the will of God. Here we see the frailty of the Messiah Man. We witness His anguish as He re-evaluated the death on the cross. He counted the cost; and grief-stricken, He pleaded for the cup to pass Him by.

"And he went a little father, and fell on his face, and prayed, saying, O my Father, if it be possible, let this cup pass from me: nevertheless not as I will, but as thou wilt."
Matthew 26:39

We see Him weigh His deepest desire against the will of the Father. For a moment, He exercised His free will as a man (His right to choose) and recoils back into the shell of God's will. This is a price too great, a death too painful. I can imagine His life flashing before Him. He lived a life free of sin-which as a man was not easy to do. He had loved with all His heart-through rejection, false accusations and threats of being stoned, and more. He had paid a dear price very step of the way. And, like a lamb to the slaughter, He had not defended Himself on His course to fulfill God's purpose. He must have thought, "Father, I am blameless. Why should I die for the sins of the world?" As He continued to pray, He could feel the gradual separation from the Father as the sins of each man that ever lived and that would ever live on the face of the earth was laid upon Him.

In tremendous distress and apprehension, He goes to check on the men, his disciples whom He had chosen to be with him at this time. Perhaps they could offer Him a degree of comfort-a way of escape from this lonely dilemma. Upon His arrival to the men, He finds them all asleep.

"Watch and pray, that ye enter not into temptation: the spirit indeed is willing, but the flesh is weak."

Matthew 26:41

Jesus was faced with the frailty of men. He encourages them to pray. Out of His own current experience, He offers a word of understanding-that the spirit indeed is willing, but the body is weak. He could identify with their weakness for He felt it, too.

81

"He went away again the second time, and prayed, saying, O my Father, if this cup may not pass away from me, except I drink it, thy will be done."

Matthew
26:42

He made His way back to pray, sweat streaming down His face. Again He tried hopelessly to exercise His rights as a man, His right to choose. He painfully prayed for God's will to be done. As the sense of separation from the Father lay heavy on His heart, sweat like blood dripped down from His face. He needed to pull this off. It was the reason for which He was sent. It was the hardest task yet. He knew He would not make it without the help of the Father. He knew the liberation of posterity, generations yet to come, depended on the "decision of the moment."

"And he left them, and went away again, and prayed the third time, saying the same words."

Matthew 26:44

Jesus did not stop there. He prayed consistently and persistently enforcing the will of the Father into manifestation. He was completely consumed by His communication with the Father. He knew so very well He could not do this alone. His humility drew Him time and again to His Father. Jesus did not pray one time or two times. He prayed the same prayer three times. Sometimes the will of God is not easy. We need to enforce it in prayer until our spirit, soul, and body are in total alignment to His will.

" 7 Who in the days of His flesh, when he had offered up prayers and supplications with strong crying and tears unto him that was able to save him from death, and was heard in that he feared; 8 though He was a son, yet learned He obedience by the things which he suffered."

Hebrews 5:7-8

Remember that even as Jesus prayed in the days of His flesh to be saved from premature death so as not to abort His mission, He prayed fervently in this time to see the death through, to prohibit the abortion of the fulfillment of His mission.

The plan of the enemy is to abort your mission. There is no option or substitute for prayer. Prayer is a necessity in the life of the Christian man and the believer. Ultimately, the prayer man survives.

PRAYER WAS THE SECRET TO JESUS' SUCCESS

The Ultimate Prayer Man walked on water, raised the dead, and opened blind eyes. He cast out devils and set the captives free. He restored broken lives. He fulfilled every iota of His ministry to the very end. Prayer was the secret to His success.

Prayer exalts God and conforms us to His will. Prayer superimposes the manifestation of the will of God into the natural realm. It is the breeding ground for signs, wonders, and miracles. Prayer protects us and releases God's glory in our lives.

Is prayer then everything? No, but realize prayer is the foundation that holds the building together. It is the core device that upholds the other equipment. It strengthens our relationship with God and, out of that relationship, emanates love, faith, and everything else we need to complete us in our Christian walk.

Prayer changes everything. It will break down the walls of racism and tear down the dividing walls of segregation. Prayer will enforce the will of God in your life. It will draw the backslider back to God. It will literally change ungodly legislations and laws in a community.

Prayer destroys the works of darkness and breaks its power of operation. Prayer will bring down kingdoms, thrones, and dominions to their knees in awe of the great God. Prayer is the key to a successful and victorious Christian life.

PWC (Prayerlessness Without Ceasing) will cost you more than a few sleepless nights. This epidemic can cost you your life, your ministry, your family, your children, your business, your job, and much more. I plead with you today to begin a consistent and intense prayer life-for yourself, for you family, for your church, for your city, community, and nation. I challenge you-no, I dare you-to pray even for the nations of the world. Your prayer has much power. You can make a difference, and you can start right where you are.

I demand, command, and decree your release from every yoke, bondage, imprisonment, and every soul tie. I command you to be untied from that which has you bound through the witness of the Blood of Christ. I declare that your soul is the Lord's. I command the chains around your hands, feet, and neck to be broken off of you. I command walls of confinement to fall. I command you to leap over walls that have resisted you all these years.

May you run through every troop in the name of Jesus. I confer upon you fresh oil, fresh power, supernatural powers of deliverance, and new beginnings. I confer upon you the miracle of divine protection, deliverance, provision, and favor.

I command new stirring of God within your spirit man. I command you to rise up and take hold of God as never before. I re-instate your prayer life and spiritual sensitivity. Before God and man, I declare that no man will take your place.

Lift your right hand pray this prayer with me:

Satan, hands off my life, my wife, my children, my home, my church, and my community!

Hands off my inheritance, my finances, my health, my progress, my focus, and my prayer life!

In Jesus' name, hands off!

I will never be the same again. I will not be denied. I will see victory. I will see the salvation of my God in Jesus' mighty name! Amen!

About the Author

Archbishop Nicholas Duncan-Williams is known in many parts of the world as the "Apostle of Prayer" and is the Presiding Archbishop and General Overseer of Christian Action Faith Ministries, with over 100 affiliate and branch churches located in North America, Europe, Asia, and Africa.

He is also the founder and President of Prayer Summit International. Anointed in the ministry of prayer, healing, and the prophetic, his teachings have touched countless lives world-wide over the past thirty years. His intense passion for intercession and strategic prayer is born out of his personal experience. Archbishop Duncan-Williams is a well sought-after speaker, dynamic preacher, and a firm believer in the truth that prayer is the key foundation upon which to build anything and that there is no substitute for prayer.

"This booklet is designed for the Christian man. It will challenge you, motivate you, and draw you back on course to your real purpose as a man.

I wrote this book to push you off the edge of complacency into spiritual warfare over our families, churches, communities, and nations. There is no substitute for prayer. Men are commanded to pray always. As heads, leaders, and seed bearers, men are under constant attack from unseen forces (spirits without bodies). All around you are unseen powers of Jezebel and Delilah, and their purpose is to control you and take you off course. Prayerlessness is one of the strategies of the enemy as the he launches his attack on the male figure. Since Jesus the Son of God prayed consistently while He was here on earth, you have no excuse."